EMOTIONAL MATURITY FOR WOMEN

***Balancing Emotions:** A Guide for Empowering Women, Navigating Feelings, Inner Strength, Self-Awareness, Embrace Growth, Strategies and Problem Solving Techniques*

Brandon Oliver

TABLE OF CONTENTS

TABLE OF CONTENTS

INTRODUCTION

CHAPTER 1

WHAT IS EMOTIONAL MATURITY?

CHARACTERISTICS OF A MATURE WOMAN

CHAPTER 2

WHAT IS SELF-AWARENESS AND HOW TO DEVELOP IT

HOW TO DEVELOP AND PRACTICE SELF-REGULATION

ENHANCING SELF-REGULATION THROUGH MINDFULNESS AND COGNITIVE

STRATEGIES

FOSTERING SELF-REGULATION IN CHILDREN AND ADULTS

HOW TO RECOGNIZE AND HANDLE THE THINGS THAT SET OFF YOUR EMOTIONS

IDENTIFYING YOUR EMOTIONAL TRIGGERS

TRACING THE ROOTS AND CURIOSITY

MANAGING TRIGGERS IN THE MOMENT

CREATING DISTANCE AND PROMOTING UNDERSTANDING IN EMOTIONAL

SITUATIONS

IDENTIFYING AND ADDRESSING TOXIC RELATIONSHIP DYNAMICS

CHAPTER 3

STRESS MANAGEMENT FOR WOMEN

CAUSES OF STRESS IN WOMEN

TYPES OF STRESS IN WOMEN: UNDERSTANDING CHRONIC STRESS

SYMPTOMS OF STRESS IN WOMEN

HEALTH EFFECTS OF STRESS ON WOMEN

STRESS MANAGEMENT TECHNIQUES

REDUCING CHRONIC STRESS

ANGER MANAGEMENT IN WOMEN

RECOGNIZING AND OWNING YOUR ANGER

SIGNS OF WOMEN'S ANGER

UNDERSTANDING YOUR ANGER PROCESS

HEALTHY WAYS TO MANAGE YOUR ANGER

CULTIVATING PATIENCE AND RESILIENCE

THE SYNERGY OF PATIENCE AND PERSEVERANCE

CHAPTER 4

BREAKING FREE FROM THE GRIP OF PEOPLE-PLEASING AND PERFECTIONISM

RECONNECT WITH YOUR AUTHENTIC SELF

PRACTICE SELF-APPROVAL

DEALING WITH GRIEF AND LOSS

TYPES AND CAUSES OF GRIEF

EFFECTS OF GRIEF

EMOTIONAL AND PHYSICAL IMPACT

COMPLICATIONS AND SUPPORT

NAVIGATING GRIEF AND SEEKING SUPPORT

WHEN TO SEEK HELP

COPING STRATEGIES

SUPPORTING A GRIEVING LOVED ONE

CHAPTER 5

HOW TO BE EMOTIONALLY MATURE IN RELATIONSHIPS

BUILDING HEALTHY RELATIONSHIPS

BENEFITS OF HEALTHY RELATIONSHIPS

EFFECTIVE COMMUNICATION IN HEALTHY RELATIONSHIPS

SUSTAINING HEALTHY RELATIONSHIPS

NURTURING HEALTHY FRIENDSHIPS

CHAPTER 6

MANAGING CONFLICT CONSTRUCTIVELY

THE 6 C'S OF CONFLICT MANAGEMENT

MANAGING CONFLICTS

DEALING WITH CRITICISM

CHAPTER 7

THE POWER OF FORGIVENESS: HOW TO LET GO AND HEAL YOUR HEART

UNDERSTANDING FORGIVENESS

THE HEALING POWER OF FORGIVENESS

STEPS TO PRACTICE FORGIVENESS

THE HEALING POWER OF FORGIVENESS FOR MENTAL AND PHYSICAL WELL-BEING

EMBRACING FORGIVENESS FOR PERSONAL GROWTH AND WELLNESS

<u>**CHAPTER 8**</u>

HOW TO NAVIGATE AND EMBRACE LIFE'S TRANSITIONS

<u>**CONCLUSION**</u>

Brandon Oliver

INTRODUCTION

Have you ever felt like you're on a rollercoaster of emotions, navigating through life's ups and downs? Well, you're not alone. In fact, that journey toward emotional maturity is something many women can relate to.

This book is a cozy corner where we're going to explore what it means to truly grow into our emotional selves. This isn't about fitting into some mold society has set for us. No, it's about finding our unique path to inner strength and peace.

Throughout these pages, we'll descend deep into what emotional maturity really entails. It's not just about keeping a stiff upper lip or suppressing feelings. It's about understanding our emotions, learning from them, and using that understanding to make better choices and live more fulfilling lives.

You'll find tips, and exercises to help you along the way. Whether you're just starting out on this journey or you've been walking it for a while, there's something here for you. So grab a cup of tea, cozy up, and let's embark on this adventure together. Here's to embracing our emotions and becoming the strong, resilient women we're meant to be!

CHAPTER 1

WHAT IS EMOTIONAL MATURITY?

Emotional maturity is a widely discussed concept in psychology because our emotions play a fundamental role in shaping our identity. When we refer to someone as emotionally mature, we are describing an individual capable of managing, regulating, and expressing their emotions in a socially acceptable manner.

Furthermore, it signifies one's natural aptitude for intelligently articulating emotions, regardless of the circumstances. It encompasses the skill to finely tune emotional responses as needed.

In simpler terms, emotional maturity refers to the capacity to effectively handle and control one's emotional reactions according to the demands of a situation. An integral aspect of this maturity involves the ability to endure stress and manage anxiety, both common occurrences in daily life. An emotionally mature individual can analyze situations calmly and make considered decisions.

Moreover, emotional maturity fosters awareness of subtle feelings that might otherwise be overlooked, preventing feelings of overwhelm and irritability during challenging times. An emotionally mature person is envisioned as serene and composed, adept at regulating emotions to prevent them from overpowering.

Emotional maturity also entails growing alongside one's feelings, mastering their management and application in social contexts. Such individuals possess self-understanding and continually work on managing their thoughts and emotions to navigate challenges effectively.

Being emotionally mature facilitates resolving conflicts and everyday issues in a healthier manner, preventing emotional turmoil from overwhelming. It is essential to recognize that emotional maturity is an ongoing process, requiring continual practice and adaptation to varying situations encountered in life.

Ultimately, emotional maturity enables individuals to navigate emotions adeptly, acknowledging discomfort and effectively coping with it without succumbing to negative emotions like anger, regret, or guilt. Adaptability and composure are vital components of emotional maturity, allowing individuals to thrive amidst unpredictable challenges and view negative emotional reactions as opportunities for personal growth and development.

Characteristics of a mature woman

1. Taking Control of Emotions

Women are often perceived as more emotionally expressive than men, leading to the stereotype of women being inherently emotional beings. Unfortunately, this perception sometimes results in women being viewed as less rational. However, being emotionally expressive does not equate to irrationality; rather, its how emotions are managed and expressed that defines rationality or irrationality.

An emotionally mature woman demonstrates significant emotional strength, commonly referred to as emotional maturity. This entails taking charge of one's emotions recognizing, interpreting, controlling, and expressing them appropriately. When faced with emotional overwhelm, a mature woman promptly adjusts her approach, focusing on correcting errors rather than justifying herself. She avoids impulsiveness in tense situations, understanding that ongoing self-evaluation is crucial for emotional well-being.

2. Embracing Different Perspectives

Another admirable trait of a mature woman is her ability to consider various viewpoints a hallmark of mental maturity. Intentionally open-minded, she assesses situations from multiple angles before forming conclusions, unlike her less mature counterparts. Immature individuals often allow ego or personal biases to obstruct understanding, prioritizing their own perspective over others'. Conversely, a mature woman questions stereotypes and groupthink, acknowledging the limitations of her understanding and embracing diverse viewpoints to foster rationality in relationships and decision-making.

3. Owning Up to Mistakes and Adjusting

A key characteristic appreciated in mature women is their capacity for self-analysis, acknowledgment of wrongdoing, and willingness to adapt. They set aside ego, apologize when necessary, and strive for fairness and rationality in actions and judgments. This humility and accountability contribute to lasting, meaningful relationships built on trust and mutual respect.

4. Adaptability

While not always thrilled about change, mature women understand its necessity and embrace adaptability. Despite initial discomfort, they recognize the benefits of adaptation and humbly engage with new challenges. This quality not only drives personal growth but also garners admiration from peers, as mature women prioritize learning and growth over complaint.

5. Realistic Expectations

Mature individuals maintain realistic expectations of themselves, avoiding inflated self-importance. They acknowledge strengths and weaknesses, leveraging them effectively while striving for excellence through dedication and effort.

6. Delayed Gratification

A mature woman prioritizes long-term goals over immediate satisfaction, demonstrating discipline and a strong work ethic. They carefully weigh the consequences of actions, prioritize tasks, and uphold values of punctuality and organization.

7. Consistency and Predictability

People find comfort in the predictability of emotionally mature women, who strive for consistency in behavior and communication. Attentive to their mental and emotional well-being, they approach situations thoughtfully and respond appropriately, fostering trust and reliability in relationships.

8. Self-Acceptance

Maturity is reflected in self-acceptance, as women come to understand and embrace their strengths and weaknesses fully. Free from the need for external validation, they establish healthy boundaries and prioritize their physical, emotional, and mental well-being.

9. Taking Responsibility

Mature women take charge of their lives, making deliberate decisions and accepting responsibility for their outcomes. They understand the importance of accountability and are committed to living purposefully, regardless of challenges or obstacles.

CHAPTER 2

WHAT IS SELF-AWARENESS AND HOW TO DEVELOP IT

Self-awareness entails the capacity to introspectively focus on one's actions, thoughts, and emotions, evaluating their alignment with personal standards. Highly self-aware individuals can objectively assess themselves, manage emotions, uphold values, and comprehend how others perceive them.

In simpler terms, individuals with high self-awareness can impartially analyze their actions, emotions, and thoughts. This skill is uncommon, as many tend to interpret situations based on emotions rather than objectivity. Developing self-awareness is crucial for leaders as it enables them to gauge their progress, effectiveness, and adapt as needed.

Self-awareness manifests in two forms: public and private.

Public self-awareness involves awareness of one's outward presentation to others, leading individuals to conform to social norms. However, excessive focus on this aspect can lead to self-consciousness, causing individuals to overly worry about others' opinions.

Private self-awareness involves introspection into one's internal state, fostering curiosity about one's feelings and reactions. For instance, recognizing physical tension before an important meeting and attributing it to anxiety demonstrates private self-awareness.

When self-awareness shifts to self-consciousness, individuals may suppress certain aspects of themselves, resulting in an inauthentic persona.

The significance of self-awareness lies in its correlation with happiness, improved relationships, personal and social control, and enhanced job satisfaction.

Enhancing self-awareness offers numerous benefits, including the ability to influence outcomes, make better decisions, communicate effectively, understand diverse perspectives, overcome biases, build stronger relationships, regulate emotions, reduce stress, and increase happiness.

Despite its prevalence in leadership discourse, only a small percentage of individuals truly embody self-awareness. Many suppress emotions due to societal expectations, leading to internalization or externalization of negative emotions, hindering personal growth.

Lack of self-awareness poses challenges in leadership, as evidenced by studies showing that as individuals ascend in leadership roles, they become more self-assured but less empathetic towards others' perspectives.

Canadian researchers found that increased power diminishes empathy and consideration for others' needs and perspectives. Such leaders often resist change themselves, expecting it from others instead.

How to develop and practice self-regulation

Self-regulation, the ability to manage behavior, emotions, and thoughts towards long-term goals, includes emotional self-regulation, the capacity to control disruptive emotions and impulses.

Developing self-regulation starts in childhood, crucial for emotional maturity and later social interactions. Maturing involves managing emotions, social situations, and cognitive challenges with patience and mindfulness.

Self-regulation is vital for navigating life's challenges, bridging the gap between feeling and action, enabling thoughtful decision-making. Lacking this skill can lead to social, emotional, and mental health issues.

Individuals skilled in self-regulation act according to values, maintain composure, persist through adversity, and adapt to situations. They can control impulses, express themselves appropriately, and find opportunities in challenges.

Cultivating self-regulation fosters resilience, enabling individuals to bounce back from failure and handle stress effectively. Research shows it correlates with positive health outcomes, including increased happiness and overall well-being.

Self-regulation issues can arise from early neglect or a lack of coping strategies. Addressing these problems early prevents escalation into serious mental health disorders or risky behaviors.

Despite its importance, many aren't taught self-regulation strategies, often assuming individuals will naturally outgrow impulsivity. However, teaching concrete strategies for self-regulation benefits both children and adults alike.

Enhancing Self-Regulation through Mindfulness and Cognitive Strategies

Mindfulness, as defined by Jon Kabat-Zinn, emphasizes purposeful, non-judgmental awareness in the present moment. Through practices like focused breathing and gratitude, mindfulness fosters distance from reactive responses, promoting focus, calmness, and relaxation.

Research underscores mindfulness's benefits, showing improvements in attention, aiding in emotional regulation and executive function enhancement.

Cognitive reappraisal, another strategy, involves reframing thoughts to alter emotional reactions. For instance, interpreting a friend's unreturned messages as busyness rather than personal rejection. Studies reveal its link to increased positive emotions and reduced negativity.

Additional effective self-regulation strategies include acceptance and problem-solving, while unproductive tactics encompass avoidance, distraction, suppression, and worrying.

Fostering Self-Regulation in Children and Adults

Parents can nurture self-regulation in children through consistent routines and teaching patience by delaying gratification. Ignoring disruptive behaviors reinforces waiting and self-control.

For adults, recognizing the power of choice in reactions to situations is pivotal. Understanding the options of approach, avoidance, and attack empowers individuals to navigate emotions effectively.

Self-awareness of emotions and bodily cues aids in identifying emotional states, facilitating timely intervention. Focusing on core values rather than transient emotions restores equilibrium.

Cultivating Self-Regulation as a Lifelong Practice

Mastering self-regulation transforms it into a habitual response, enhancing resilience in adversity. Seeking professional guidance is advisable if self-regulation proves challenging, as therapists can tailor strategies to individual needs and offer a supportive environment for skill development.

How to recognize and handle the things that set off your emotions

Throughout any given day, a myriad of emotions may arise, ranging from excitement to unease, each often tied to specific events or interactions. These emotional responses can vary depending on one's mindset and the context of the situation.

Emotional triggers, irrespective of one's current emotional state, are elements such as memories, experiences, or events that incite intense emotional reactions. They are notably associated with conditions like post-traumatic stress disorder (PTSD), making it essential to recognize and address them for emotional well-being.

Identifying Your Emotional Triggers
Emotional triggers are unique to each individual, encompassing reminders of unwanted memories, uncomfortable topics, or

others' words and actions. Common triggers include experiences of rejection, betrayal, unjust treatment, or loss of control.

Listening to both mental and physical cues is pivotal in recognizing triggers. Symptoms like a racing heart or upset stomach can signal an emotional response, prompting introspection into the situation at hand.

Tracing the Roots and Curiosity

When confronted with triggers, tracing the feelings back to their origins can provide insight into their underlying causes. Reflecting on past experiences that evoke similar emotions can help identify patterns and understand the present reaction.

Approaching triggers with curiosity rather than avoidance allows for deeper exploration. By acknowledging and examining these emotions, one can uncover connections and better manage their responses.

Managing Triggers in the Moment

While avoiding triggering situations may seem appealing, it's often impractical. Instead, owning and accepting one's feelings in the moment is crucial. Recognizing that past experiences may influence current emotions fosters self-compassion and empowers active choice in response.

For instance, if a seemingly innocuous question triggers anxiety due to past teasing, acknowledging the difference between past and present circumstances can facilitate a mindful response. Choosing to engage with the situation positively, despite past pain, allows for emotional regulation and personal growth.

Creating Distance and Promoting Understanding in Emotional Situations

Taking a step back physically can be a powerful tool in preventing emotional overwhelm. Excusing yourself briefly provides an opportunity to avoid impulsive reactions, allowing for a calmer response later. Utilizing breathing or grounding techniques during this time aids in self-soothing and regaining composure, enabling a more productive approach to the situation upon return.

Maintaining an open-minded perspective is essential. Recognizing that most people do not intentionally aim to cause distress can foster empathy and understanding. Their actions may stem from their own emotional triggers or external factors unknown to you. Acknowledging the complexity of emotions individuals carry helps in interpreting behavior more accurately and empathetically.

Communication serves as a crucial tool in addressing emotional triggers in relationships. Expressing feelings using "I-statements" and employing healthy communication techniques fosters understanding and prevents future misunderstandings. Challenging the other person to engage in better communication practices can also facilitate mutual respect and empathy.

Long-term resolution of emotional triggers involves addressing their root causes. Mindfulness practices enhance awareness of present emotions, aiding in identifying triggers and developing effective coping mechanisms. Research indicates that mindfulness meditation enhances emotional processing and regulation, offering a path towards long-term emotional well-being. Engaging in various forms of meditation further cultivates inner calm and resilience, empowering individuals to navigate challenging emotions with grace and self-awareness.

Identifying and Addressing Toxic Relationship Dynamics

Recognizing and addressing toxic relationship patterns is essential for emotional well-being. In such dynamics, individuals may disregard your emotional boundaries, causing distress and harm. Below are some steps to identify and manage these patterns:

1. Establish Boundaries: Healthy relationships are built on mutual respect for boundaries. If someone consistently disregards your boundaries despite your communication, it may signal a toxic dynamic. For instance, if a friend repeatedly brings up uncomfortable topics despite your requests to avoid them, it could indicate a lack of respect for your emotional well-being.

2. Keep a Mood Journal: Tracking emotions and triggers in a journal can unveil patterns and vulnerabilities. By identifying specific triggers, such as feeling ignored by a partner, you can develop strategies to address them constructively. For instance, instead of shutting down during such situations, you might resolve to initiate a conversation with your partner about your feelings.

3. Seek Professional Help: Emotion regulation can be challenging, especially when triggers are deeply ingrained. Therapy provides a supportive environment to explore and address triggers effectively. A therapist can help you identify triggering situations, understand their underlying causes, and develop healthier coping mechanisms. Additionally, therapy offers guidance in improving communication skills and healing past traumas contributing to trigger responses.

4. Cultivate Self-Awareness: Learning to recognize and manage emotional triggers takes time and effort but yields significant benefits for relationships and overall well-being. By mastering trigger management, individuals can navigate tense situations with greater ease and minimize unnecessary distress.

In summary, addressing toxic relationship patterns involves establishing boundaries, tracking emotions, seeking professional help when needed, and cultivating self-awareness. Through these steps, individuals can foster healthier relationships and enhance their emotional well-being.

CHAPTER 3

STRESS MANAGEMENT FOR WOMEN

We can all understand the sensation of being overwhelmed; it's a universal feeling that impacts individuals regardless of age, gender, or background.

Nevertheless, stress can often remain unnoticed in women because they tend to exhibit and interpret stress symptoms differently from men. For instance, women may experience chronic pain, autoimmune conditions, depression, and anxiety disorders as manifestations of stress.

Hence, we aim to help you identify signs of stress in women and understand its effects on women's health, empowering you to take action against it. Continue reading to learn more.

Causes of stress in women

Stress typically stems from various external and internal factors. Women frequently encounter work-related stressors like long hours, heavy workloads, interpersonal conflicts, and a lack of control over job tasks.

Financial strain exacerbates stress, arising from low income, job loss, unexpected expenses, and the overarching cost of living crisis.

Additionally, familial and relational challenges, including caregiving duties, relationship discord, and parenting struggles, contribute to stress in women. Predictably, traumatic events like divorce, illness, and loss also induce stress.

Moreover, hormonal influences such as menopause can compound stress, with its symptoms intensifying stress levels and vice versa.

Types of stress in women: understanding chronic stress

Stress isn't a uniform experience; women encounter various types of stress, often simultaneously. These may include:

Acute stress, which arises briefly in response to specific events like work deadlines or traffic congestion.

Episodic acute stress happens when someone experiences repeated acute stress episodes, which can result in chronic stress patterns.

Chronic stress, a prolonged form resulting from ongoing, uncontrollable stressors. Notably, research suggests women are 30% more likely than men to experience chronic stress.

Recognizing the signs and symptoms of stress types is crucial for pinpointing causes and addressing them effectively.

Chronic stress, in particular, poses severe physical and mental health repercussions further details on these effects follow.

Symptoms of stress in women

Stress manifests in various ways, broadly categorized as physical and mental symptoms.

Physical symptoms stem from the body's stress response, involving hormone release such as cortisol and adrenaline. This triggers a 'fight or flight' mode, increasing heart rate, blood pressure, and respiration.

Despite the triggering factors not being necessarily life-threatening, the body's response can become chronic, leading to physical symptoms such as headaches, muscle tension, digestive issues, fatigue, appetite changes, sleep disturbances, rapid heartbeat, susceptibility to illnesses, and menstrual irregularities.

Mental symptoms arise from chronic stress impacting areas of the brain responsible for emotional regulation, potentially leading to decreased coping abilities and increased risks of anxiety, depression, and PTSD.

Additional mental symptoms of chronic stress encompass:

- Anxiety, apprehension, or jitteriness
- Irritability or outbursts of anger
- Challenges with concentration or decision-making
- Sensations of feeling inundated or incapable of managing situations.
- Diminished self-esteem or feelings of insignificance
- Persistent sadness or depression
- Fluctuations in mood

- Withdrawal from social interactions or increased isolation
- Alterations in appetite or sleep patterns
- Reliance on substances or alternative unhealthy strategies for coping.

Health effects of stress on women

The combined impact of chronic stress, both physical and mental, can significantly affect women's overall health in several ways:

Cardiovascular issues: Chronic stress can elevate cortisol levels, leading to heightened blood pressure and cholesterol, thereby increasing the likelihood of heart disease, stroke, and other cardiovascular problems.

Digestive disturbances: Stress response can hinder digestion, resulting in conditions like irritable bowel syndrome (IBS), stomach ulcers, and acid reflux.

Reproductive challenges: Prolonged stress may disrupt menstrual cycles, fertility, and potentially lead to premature menopause. It could also elevate the risk of pregnancy complications such as premature births and low birth weight.

Weakened immune system: Suppression of normal bodily functions due to stress can compromise the immune system, rendering women more susceptible to infections and illnesses.

Skin ailments: Stress exacerbates skin conditions such as acne, eczema, and psoriasis.

Stress management techniques
Effective stress management involves integrating daily stress-reducing practices rather than just addressing crises. These techniques may include:

Regular exercise: Physical activity releases endorphins, promoting mood improvement and stress relief.

Relaxation methods: Deep breathing exercises, meditation, and yoga foster relaxation and decrease stress levels.

Time management: Prioritizing tasks and setting realistic goals aids in alleviating feelings of overwhelm and stress.

Social support: Spending time with loved ones and engaging in enjoyable activities foster happiness and connection, reducing stress levels.

Self-care: Engaging in pleasurable and relaxing activities like reading, bathing, or receiving a massage helps reduce stress.

Healthy lifestyle habits: Maintaining a balanced diet, sufficient sleep, and moderate alcohol and caffeine consumption promotes overall wellbeing and reduces stress levels.

Reducing chronic stress

Addressing chronic stress entails identifying its sources, possibly through journaling to recognize triggers and patterns. Incorporating relaxation techniques into daily life and prioritizing self-care are crucial steps. Setting boundaries and learning to decline unrealistic demands can aid in long-term stress reduction. Seeking professional assistance is advisable if chronic stress significantly impacts daily functioning, as mental health professionals can offer support and coping strategies.

Anger management in women

Women experience anger differently from men, often expressing it indirectly rather than overtly. Instead of outward aggression, unresolved anger in women may manifest as resentment, depression, strained relationships, or passive-aggressive behavior.

If you find it challenging to manage your anger and it's impacting your life negatively, assistance is available. We can guide you in understanding and expressing your anger healthily while helping you realize that feeling angry isn't something to be ashamed of or feel guilty about. Join us on a journey of growth, healing, and self-improvement.

Recognizing and Owning Your Anger

Many women have been conditioned to suppress their anger, making it difficult to recognize when they are angry. Sometimes, anger only becomes apparent after the situation has passed. However, acknowledging and being aware of your anger is crucial to managing it effectively. Anger management for women offers personalized approaches to address this issue

Signs of Women's Anger

Indicators that you might be experiencing anger include insomnia, depression, anxiety, substance misuse, overspending, overeating, crying, resentment, relationship difficulties, and passive-aggressive behavior. Owning your anger involves acknowledging and taking responsibility for it, a process that can be facilitated with support.

Understanding Your Anger Process

Anger management for women involves understanding your individual anger processes. Becoming attuned to your emotions helps you identify patterns and make better choices. The anger process typically comprises four stages:

1. **Triggers:** These are unique to each person and can include threatening behavior, attacks, feeling invalidated or treated unfairly, disrespect, frustration, powerlessness, and

stress. Identifying your triggers aids in recognizing and managing anger.

2. Escalation: Anger-related feelings intensify during this stage. It's essential to express anger healthily before it becomes overwhelming.

3. Explosion: Uncontrolled anger may lead to angry outbursts, damaging personal or professional relationships.

4. Post-Explosion: Dealing with the aftermath involves repairing relationships and addressing consequences. Anger management empowers women to express anger constructively before it escalates.

Learning to navigate your anger process effectively can enhance your emotional well-being and interpersonal relationships. With guidance and support, you can develop healthy ways to express and manage your anger, promoting personal growth and fulfillment.

Healthy Ways to Manage Your Anger

Anger management for women doesn't advocate for suppressing anger but rather encourages constructive expression or redirection of anger towards positive outcomes. Here are some tips and strategies to help manage anger effectively:

1. Self-awareness: Understand your identity, values, and how you typically express emotions, including anger. This self-awareness forms the foundation for managing anger.

2. Address basic needs: Ensure your fundamental needs are met, such as hunger, thirst, and rest. Unmet needs can trigger anger, so tune into your physical and emotional requirements.

3. Pause before speaking: When angered, refrain from immediate verbal reactions. Take time to compose your thoughts, allowing others the same opportunity for reflection.

4. Express concerns calmly: Communicate your grievances once you've regained composure. Aim for a peaceful and rational dialogue, ensuring your message is heard effectively.

5. Establish boundaries: Define healthy boundaries to maintain emotional distance while engaging with the source of anger, preserving your well-being.

6. Engage in physical activity: Exercise releases tension and reduces anger. Whether it's hitting the gym, dancing, or enjoying outdoor walks, physical movement promotes emotional balance.

7. Acceptance of control: Acknowledge what you can and cannot control, fostering acceptance and facilitating anger release. Redirect focus towards aspects within your control for constructive change.

8. Problem-solving approach: Channel anger energy into problem-solving. Once in a calmer state, brainstorm solutions to address underlying issues, fostering personal growth and resolution.

9. Visualize a traffic light: Use the traffic light analogy to gauge emotional intensity. Green signifies calmness, yellow signals escalating frustration, and red prompts immediate cessation to prevent outbursts.

10. Stress management: Prioritize stress reduction techniques to mitigate anger triggers. Managing stress equips you with better emotional regulation skills, facilitating effective anger management.

Incorporating these strategies into your routine empowers you to navigate anger more healthily, promoting emotional well-being and constructive conflict resolution.

Cultivating patience and resilience

In today's world, characterized by instant gratification and rapid pace, patience is often overlooked as a valuable virtue. However, embracing patience holds the key to unlocking numerous mental and emotional benefits.

Foremost, patience allows us to cultivate emotional resilience, enabling better management of emotions and reactions, especially in challenging situations. This resilience is vital for nurturing healthy relationships and overcoming obstacles effectively.

Moreover, patience enhances our focus and decision-making skills. By taking time to deliberate on choices, we make more informed decisions that serve us well in the long term. Patience fosters strategic thinking, reducing impulsivity and promoting thoughtful action.

Perseverance: Sustaining Momentum amidst Challenges

In the face of adversity, it's natural to feel disheartened, yet true strength lies in perseverance, the ability to persist despite setbacks. Perseverance serves as the driving force propelling us towards our goals.

An important outcome of perseverance is the cultivation of self-motivation. Committing to completing tasks instills discipline and prioritization, translating into increased efficiency and goal attainment across various areas of life.

Additionally, perseverance teaches adaptability, essential for navigating obstacles and embracing change. This adaptability empowers us to confront new challenges with resilience and flexibility.

The Synergy of Patience and Perseverance

When patience and perseverance work in harmony, they create a formidable combination fostering inner fortitude and personal development. Perseverance propels us forward with determination and self-discipline, while patience provides emotional stability to overcome hurdles.

Though developing these virtues demands intentional effort and practice, the rewards are substantial. Embracing patience and perseverance not only fuels personal growth but also unveils our true potential, inspiring others to do the same.

Cultivating these virtues is a transformative journey, enriching our lives with resilience, strength, and grace. As we harness the power of patience and perseverance, we embody the essence of true resilience, paving the way for a more empowered and fulfilling existence.

CHAPTER 4

BREAKING FREE FROM THE GRIP OF PEOPLE-PLEASING AND PERFECTIONISM

What Factors Contribute to Women's Vulnerability to People-Pleasing and Perfectionism?

Although people-pleasing and perfectionism aren't exclusively experienced by women, societal norms often shape women to prioritize caregiving, accommodate others' needs before their own, and adopt a passive demeanor. The fear of being labeled as difficult or high maintenance leads many women to prioritize others' opinions over their own well-being, often agreeing to demands without asserting their own boundaries.

In many cultures, women grapple with the conflicting expectations of excelling in both motherhood and professional spheres. The ideal of having it all places immense pressure on women to juggle multiple roles flawlessly, without seeking assistance or showing any signs of struggle. Consequently, women who lean towards perfectionism link their self-worth to their achievements, whether in their roles as mothers, employees, volunteers, or athletes.

Remember, Your Value Isn't Defined Solely by Your Achievements.

Both people-pleasing and perfectionism stem from a deep-seated fear of inadequacy and a desire for external validation. This constant need to please and strive for perfection creates a cycle where no amount of effort seems enough. It's crucial to recognize that perfection is unattainable, and the quest to please everyone is equally futile.

Your Identity Is Not Determined by Others' Perceptions.

Focusing solely on pleasing others creates a disconnection between your authentic self and the persona you present to the world. Seeking validation from external sources may garner temporary approval, but it fails to address the underlying self-doubt and anxiety. True acceptance comes from embracing your genuine self, rather than conforming to others' expectations.

Reconnect with Your Authentic Self

People-pleasing and perfectionism act as barriers that obscure your true identity. By constantly striving to meet others' expectations, you lose sight of your own preferences, beliefs, and values. Engage in self-exploration gradually, allowing yourself the freedom to evolve and grow over time.

Practice Self-Approval

Relying solely on others' approval for self-worth is unsustainable. Cultivating self-compassion and positive self-talk enables you to diminish the need for external validation. By nurturing a sense of self-acceptance, you become less dependent on others' opinions for validation and fulfillment.

Dealing with grief and loss

Grief is the natural emotional reaction to the departure of someone significant, like a family member or friend, or in response to other significant losses such as serious illness or divorce.

It often involves deep sadness, shock, numbness, or even denial and anger. Over time, grief tends to lessen in intensity, though it can still linger and affect individuals differently.

Grief is a unique journey for each person, often exhausting and emotionally draining, which may hinder daily activities. Coping mechanisms vary; some become more active, while others prefer privacy in dealing with their emotions.

There is no universal pattern for grief expression, as it differs across cultures. Despite the pain, most individuals find that with time, grief diminishes, allowing for the rediscovery of joy and purpose. Some even gain new insights and strength from their loss.

Types and Causes of Grief

Grief isn't solely tied to death but can stem from various significant losses, with intensity correlating to the significance of the loss. Examples include:

- Death of a loved one, which can be especially severe in cases of infant or child loss or suicide.

- Divorce or separation.

- Loss of a cherished pet.

- Surrendering something of importance.

- Work-related changes like unemployment, retirement, or retrenchment.

- Diagnosis of terminal illness.

- Deteriorating health due to illness, accident, or disability.

- Miscarriage, infertility, or challenges with childbirth.

- Having a child with special needs or facing familial challenges.

- Relocation or separation from loved ones.

- Adapting to an empty nest following the departure of children from home.

Effects of Grief

Grief can evoke intense and overwhelming emotions, sometimes leading to feelings of depression. In the immediate aftermath of loss, individuals may experience shock, denial, sadness, loneliness, anger, or guilt. These feelings can be relentless and may come in waves, but with time, they typically ease.

Grief manifests differently in individuals. Common reactions include sadness, shock, denial, numbness, anger, guilt, blame, or relief.

Emotional and Physical Impact

Grieving individuals may struggle with concentration, withdrawal from usual activities, substance use, and suicidal thoughts. Physically, grief can lead to exhaustion, weakened immunity, changes in appetite and weight, sleep disturbances, and various bodily discomforts.

Spiritual Reflection and Post-Traumatic Growth

Grief often prompts introspection and spiritual exploration, with some experiencing dreams or seeking deeper meaning in their beliefs. Despite the pain, some individuals may emerge from grief with newfound wisdom, maturity, and purpose in life.

Complications and Support

For some, grief can be prolonged or intensified, hindering daily functioning. This may be more likely after traumatic losses, leading to complicated grief or depression, characterized by persistent sorrow and emotional paralysis. In such cases, seeking professional support is crucial for coping and healing.

Navigating Grief and Seeking Support

Experiencing grief can lead to confusion, overwhelming sadness, extreme thoughts, and behaviors, as well as a persistent longing for the past. Prolonged grief may result in a fixation on memories of the deceased, making the future appear bleak.

When to Seek Help

Persistent feelings of sadness and despair, accompanied by an inability to find joy, could indicate depression. If grief starts to interfere significantly with daily life, seeking professional help is crucial. Indications that you might require support include struggles with socializing, sleep disturbances, alterations in appetite, intense and persistent emotions, and thoughts of self-harm.

Coping Strategies

While grief may always linger to some extent, over time, the intense pain typically subsides, making it easier to cope. Below are some coping mechanisms:

1. Allow yourself to grieve: Crying and expressing emotions are natural parts of the process. Spending time alone, listening to music, or writing can aid in emotional release.

2. Live one day at a time: Establishing a regular routine, engaging in self-care activities, and avoiding major decisions in the first year after a loss can provide stability and comfort.

3. Seek help: Talking to a doctor, joining support groups, or confiding in trusted friends or family members can provide valuable support.

4. Stay connected: Surround yourself with supportive individuals who can offer comfort and companionship.

5. Create positive memories: Honor the life of the deceased through rituals, writing, or sharing stories with others.

6. Prioritize health: Regular exercise, nutritious eating, adequate sleep, and avoiding substance abuse contribute to overall well-being.

7. Navigate anniversaries: Recognize special occasions with simple ceremonies or gatherings to acknowledge the significance of those dates.

Supporting a Grieving Loved One

If someone you care about is grieving, here are ways to offer support:

1. Initiate contact: Reach out and be available to spend time together, respecting their need for different forms of support.

2. Listen: Provide a compassionate ear without offering unsolicited advice or clichés.

Encourage conversations about the deceased if they find it comforting.

3. Engage in activities together: Participate in ordinary yet positive activities to provide companionship and distraction.

4. Offer practical help: Assist with daily tasks like cooking or childcare to alleviate some of their burdens.

5. Be mindful: Remember that grief may persist for a long time, and acknowledge important dates like birthdays or anniversaries.

Common Questions

• How long does grief last? There's no fixed timeframe for grieving, as it varies from person to person. It's essential to allow oneself time to process and not rush the healing process.

• How do I move on? Instead of moving on, focus on adapting to life without the person while honoring their memory. Moving forward doesn't mean forgetting; it means learning to live with grief as a part of life's journey.

CHAPTER 5

HOW TO BE EMOTIONALLY MATURE IN RELATIONSHIPS

Developing emotional maturity in relationships requires the ability to relinquish dependence and cultivate self-empowerment. Surprisingly, this skill can be acquired through learning. Here are key practices you can implement today to foster emotional maturity and cultivate more fulfilling, intimate connections:

1. Assume Responsibility for Your Needs

Many individuals enter relationships with the expectation that their partner will fulfill all their needs, whether for social interaction, emotional support, or familial connection. Some even rely on their partner for financial or sexual fulfillment without clearly communicating their needs. Emotional maturity involves recognizing that it's natural to have needs that won't always be fully met by one person alone. It means articulating your needs clearly and updating your partner as they evolve.

2. Seek Out Resources to Fulfill Your Needs

Rather than placing the burden of meeting all your needs on your partner, build a network of support to fulfill them. If your interests diverge from your partner's, cultivate relationships with others who share your passions. Similarly, establish connections with individuals who can provide emotional support in times when your partner may be unavailable or unable to meet your needs fully. Regarding sexual fulfillment, assess whether your relationship is monogamous or open, and make decisions accordingly.

3. Take Ownership of Your Feelings

Emotional maturity entails acknowledging and accepting your feelings without judgment or suppression. Many people either ignore their emotions or try to control them, which ultimately influences their decision-making. Begin practicing mindfulness by recognizing your emotions in the moment and refraining from criticism or denial. Share your feelings vulnerably with your loved ones to maintain connection.

4. Validate Your Feelings

Recognize the validity of your emotions, understanding that they may stem from past experiences rather than immediate circumstances. When experiencing intense reactions, consider whether they trigger underlying pain or trauma. Avoid attributing these reactions solely to your partner's actions and acknowledge that everyone carries emotional baggage. Additionally, accept that your partner may not always share your feelings, especially in the early stages of a relationship.

5. Take Ownership of Your Choices

Transition from a mindset of dependency to one of self-empowerment by acknowledging that your choices shape your life. Instead of waiting for your partner to change to improve your happiness, recognize that you have the agency to make decisions that align with your well-being. Avoid placing blame on your partner for your dissatisfaction and take responsibility for your own choices. This shift empowers you to evaluate whether your current situation aligns with your desires and values, leading to greater acceptance of your partner as they are.

6. Embrace Your Partner's Authenticity

During a session with a couple seeking relationship guidance, they referred to each other as future Ben and future Alexis, anticipating that their relationship would improve once they evolved into these idealized versions of themselves.

If you find yourself waiting for your partner to transform into someone different, it's essential to confront the need for acceptance. While individuals may evolve, fundamental personality traits tend to remain constant, and changing habits requires significant internal motivation over time.

To foster mutual empowerment, it's crucial to embrace your partner (and yourself) for who you both truly are. This might entail experiencing some initial disappointment as you let go of expectations, but it can lead to deeper intimacy by allowing you to fully engage with the person in front of you. Emotional maturity in relationships involves cultivating understanding, with acceptance serving as its foundation.

7. Consider Reframing Your Relationship Dynamics

Once you've embraced your partner's authenticity, you may contemplate whether you genuinely want to continue choosing them as they are. Reflect on whether any aspects of the relationship, including your partner's expectations of you, are sustainable in the long term.

If you decide to remain committed to your partner, that's commendable. However, if you realize that the relationship is no longer viable for you, consider reconfiguring it rather than immediately severing ties. Explore alternative arrangements that prioritize connection while alleviating any ongoing distress.

Building healthy relationships

Establishing and maintaining healthy relationships with your partner and family members can enrich your life and contribute to everyone's sense of well-being. However, these relationships don't spontaneously occur; they require dedicated effort and time to develop and nurture. The level of positivity you invest in a relationship directly correlates with its health and strength.

Identifying the Characteristics of a Healthy Relationship:

A healthy relationship is characterized by mutual love and support, both emotionally and practically, through good times and bad. Key elements include respect, trust, open communication, equality, shared and individual interests, understanding, honesty, care, emotional support, and alignment on important matters like finances and child-rearing.

Benefits of Healthy Relationships

Individuals in healthy relationships tend to experience greater happiness and life satisfaction while being less susceptible to physical and mental health issues. These relationships foster a sense of belonging, boost confidence, encourage personal growth, and alleviate feelings of loneliness.

Effective Communication in Healthy Relationships

Regular and attentive communication is vital in maintaining a healthy relationship. Clear expression of thoughts and active listening help prevent misunderstandings that can lead to hurt or confusion. Encouraging open dialogue involves dedicating uninterrupted time to communicate, empathizing with each other's perspectives, and avoiding assumptions. Non-verbal cues such as body language and tone also play a significant role in effective communication.

Sustaining Healthy Relationships
Continuously nurturing relationships with partners, friends, and family members is essential for overall well-being. This entails clear expression of desires through assertive communication, apologizing when necessary, demonstrating affection and appreciation, prioritizing the relationship amidst other commitments, fostering shared interests, nurturing self-esteem, and maintaining connections with friends. Addressing conflicts with mutual respect and compromise, planning for the future together, and dedicating time for family activities further contribute to relationship health and longevity.

Nurturing healthy friendships

Amidst the whirlwind of academic pursuits and extracurricular activities that define the university experience, it's easy to overlook the significance of nurturing healthy friendships. Putting Mental Health Awareness close, it's crucial to reflect on how strong friendships contribute to our emotional well-being and explore strategies to cultivate and sustain them.

Understanding the Value of Friendship

Human beings are inherently social creatures, and friendships play a vital role in our lives by providing a sense of belonging, support, and understanding. Strong bonds with friends offer emotional solace, reduce stress, and enhance overall mental health by fostering feelings of acceptance and value.

Providing Essential Emotional Support

Navigating the challenges of university life can be daunting, but having friends who understand the unique experiences and pressures of student life can offer invaluable emotional support. Healthy friendships serve as a safe space to share thoughts, seek advice, and vent frustrations, ultimately alleviating stress and anxiety.

Combatting Loneliness and Isolation

Transitioning to university, particularly for those in new environments or away from home, can lead to feelings of loneliness and isolation. Cultivating healthy friendships creates a supportive community that combats these negative emotions, fostering a sense of belonging and camaraderie.

Fostering Collaboration and Growth

University friendships provide opportunities for collaboration, intellectual exchange, and personal growth. Engaging in group activities, studying together, and participating in extracurricular pursuits with friends can enhance creativity, problem-solving skills, and academic achievement.

Building Resilience

Life's inevitable challenges become more manageable with a strong support system of friends who provide encouragement, motivation, and different perspectives. Through shared experiences, friendships contribute to resilience, empowering individuals to navigate difficulties and emerge stronger.

Tips for Nurturing Healthy Friendships

• Practice active listening and genuine interest in your friends' thoughts and feelings.

• Create an approachable atmosphere that encourages open communication and interaction.

• Participate in group activities to expand your social circle and meet like-minded individuals.

• Cultivate empathy by understanding and validating your friends' experiences without judgment.

• Build trust through reliability, honesty, and keeping promises.

• Foster open communication, sharing thoughts, feelings, and concerns openly.

• Express gratitude and appreciation for your friends' support and presence in your life.

• Make spending quality time together a priority, even when your schedules are hectic.

• Encourage self-care and well-being practices among friends.

• Embrace diversity and respect differing opinions to create an inclusive and supportive environment.

Finally, As Mental Health Awareness reminds us of the importance of prioritizing emotional well-being, let us recognize the profound impact that healthy friendships have on our life journey. By nurturing these connections, we not only enhance our own mental health but also contribute to a supportive and inclusive community where everyone thrives.

CHAPTER 6

MANAGING CONFLICT CONSTRUCTIVELY

Conflict management refers to the ability to identify and address conflicts in a sensible, fair, and efficient manner. It involves handling disagreements or perceived incompatibilities arising from differing opinions, objectives, or needs.

In a business setting, conflicts are a natural occurrence, and it's crucial to have individuals who understand how to manage and resolve them effectively. In today's competitive market, where employees strive to demonstrate their value to their companies, conflicts among team members can arise frequently.

Common Conflict Management Styles

1. Collaborating: This style aims for the best long-term results but is often the most challenging and time-consuming to achieve. It involves considering the needs and desires of all parties involved and finding a solution that satisfies everyone, known as a win-win outcome. Collaboration typically requires all parties to engage in open discussion and negotiation. It's employed when preserving relationships among parties is crucial or when the solution will have a significant impact.

2. Competing: In this style, one party refuses to compromise and insists on their own opinions or desires, disregarding those of others. This approach is adopted when certain principles or time constraints demand a specific course of action or when making an unpopular decision. Although competition can efficiently address conflicts, it also poses the potential to diminish morale and productivity.

3. Avoiding: Avoidance entails reducing conflict by either ignoring it, removing the conflicting parties from the situation, or evading it altogether. This might involve temporarily removing dissenting team members from a project, postponing deadlines, or reassigning individuals to different roles. Avoidance can be effective when a cooling-off period is needed or when additional time is required to assess the conflict. However, it should not substitute for genuine conflict resolution efforts, as unresolved conflicts may escalate into larger issues in the future.

Conflict management involves handling conflicts in a sensible, fair, and efficient manner. In a business context, where conflicts are natural, it's crucial to understand and utilize various conflict management styles. These styles include:

4. Accommodating: This style prioritizes the needs of the other party over one's own. It involves letting the other party 'win' and have their way, especially when the issue at hand is less important to the resolver. Accommodation is about maintaining peace, conserving time, and choosing battles wisely. While it may appear weak, accommodation can swiftly resolve minor conflicts and allow focus on more critical matters. However, it may lead to resentment if overused.

5. Compromising: Compromising seeks a middle ground where both parties give up some aspects of their desires to reach an agreement. Often termed lose-lose, this style requires concessions from both sides for resolution, especially in time-sensitive situations or when perfection isn't feasible.

Compromise can foster resentment if relied upon excessively but is valuable when parties are willing to make sacrifices for resolution.

The 6 C's of Conflict Management

1. Communication: Establish clear channels of communication for all parties to express their viewpoints openly, fostering understanding and preventing miscommunication.

2. Collaboration: Seek mutually beneficial outcomes through cooperation and creative problem-solving, prioritizing shared goals over individual interests.

3. Compromise: Find a middle ground between opposing views, where both sides make concessions for resolution, acknowledging that complete satisfaction for everyone may not be achievable.

4. Control: Maintain emotional composure to prevent conflicts from escalating, managing emotions for rational decision-making and conflict resolution.

5. Civility: Approach conflicts with politeness and empathy, refraining from disrespectful behavior to foster constructive discourse and resolution.

6. Commitment: Dedicate time and effort to resolving conflicts, ensuring implementation and follow-up to prevent future issues.

Managing Conflicts

1. Be aware of conflicts and address them promptly, avoiding the temptation to ignore or postpone resolution.

2. Take a considerate and rational approach, remaining calm and impartial, and investigating the situation thoroughly.

3. Decide on the appropriate course of action, considering the severity of the conflict, organizational policies, and legal implications.

4. Facilitate open communication and dialogue among parties, allowing everyone to express their viewpoints and concerns.

5. Identify options and seek agreement on a way forward, encouraging compromise and negotiation to reach a satisfactory resolution.

6. Implement agreed-upon solutions, ensuring clarity and personal responsibility among involved parties.

7. Evaluate the effectiveness of the resolution over time, addressing any recurring issues or concerns promptly.

By employing these conflict management strategies and principles, organizations can effectively navigate conflicts and foster a positive and productive work environment.

Implement Preventative Strategies for the Future

Reflect on the conflict and extract valuable lessons from the handling process. Identify areas for improvement and contemplate how conflict management skills can be enhanced. Consider pursuing training or professional development opportunities in areas such as influencing, mediation, or dispute resolution, either for yourself or a colleague.

Broaden the scope to examine the organizational context and identify actions to enhance working relationships and foster a culture of open communication and collaboration. Encourage a sense of group identity and align employees towards a common goal to mitigate future conflicts effectively.

Evaluate the need for an organizational conflict management process or mediation framework. Assess whether systemic issues within the unit contribute to recurring conflicts and explore strategies to address them systematically. Engage in conflict management practices that promote proactive resolution and cultivate a harmonious work environment.

Dealing with criticism

Research suggests that women may be more sensitive to criticism compared to men, possibly due to their heightened ability to perceive and interpret emotions, even subtle forms of criticism. While sensitivity to criticism isn't inherently negative, it can become problematic if it inhibits personal growth and development. Societal expectations regarding women's appearance and behavior further exacerbate this sensitivity, making it challenging for women to accept and address criticism constructively.

The discomfort and discouragement stemming from criticism may lead women to avoid pursuing endeavors that could potentially attract criticism, depriving them of opportunities for personal fulfillment and achievement. To overcome these challenges and continue pursuing fulfilling activities, women must learn how to effectively manage and respond to criticism.

Below are three rapid strategies for handling criticism:

1. Recognize the Source:

Instead of immediately internalizing criticism as a personal failure, consider its origin and context. Criticism often reflects the perspectives and biases of the critic, rather than inherent flaws in oneself. By understanding the source of criticism, women can extract valuable insights for self-improvement while disregarding unjustified negativity.

2. Timing Matters:

Resist the urge to address every criticism immediately. Sometimes, it's beneficial to set aside feedback temporarily and continue pursuing goals while maintaining motivation and enthusiasm. Remember that even successful individuals have imperfections, and perseverance is key to eventual success.

3. Challenge Negative Beliefs:

Criticism can trigger negative beliefs about oneself, leading to self-doubt and discouragement. Combat these negative beliefs by creating positive affirmations or counterarguments that affirm one's worth and capabilities. Over time, consistently reaffirming these positive beliefs can help women overcome self-limiting beliefs and embrace constructive criticism as a catalyst for growth.

Ultimately, while criticism may initially evoke discomfort and fear, it is a necessary component of personal and professional development. By learning to manage and respond to criticism effectively, women can harness its potential to enhance self-awareness, resilience, and overall growth.

CHAPTER 7

THE POWER OF FORGIVENESS: HOW TO LET GO AND HEAL YOUR HEART

Are you holding onto feelings of anger, resentment, or pain? It's time to free yourself from these negative emotions and explore the transformative power of forgiveness. This piece discusses the importance of forgiveness and offers strategies to let go of negativity and mend your heart.

Forgiveness doesn't mean approving of someone's actions or forgetting what happened. Instead, it's a choice to release those negative emotions and regain your inner peace. Research shows that practicing forgiveness can positively impact both mental and physical health, reducing stress and strengthening relationships.

We'll guide you through practical steps to nurture forgiveness, like recognizing how unforgiveness affects your life, changing your perspective, and showing yourself compassion. By embracing forgiveness, you can break free from pain and begin a journey toward inner healing.

Whether you're forgiving others or yourself, this guide gives you the tools and insights to start a forgiveness journey and experience its profound healing effects. Prepare to let go, heal your heart, and cultivate a more peaceful and fulfilling life.

Understanding Forgiveness

Forgiveness isn't about excusing behavior or forgetting what happened. It's a deliberate choice to release negative emotions and regain peace of mind. It's about letting go of pain and resentment that might be holding you back. When you forgive, you're not pardoning the person who hurt you; you're freeing yourself from the weight of that hurt.

Forgiveness is a process that involves acknowledging pain, understanding its impact, and choosing to let go. It requires courage and strength, but the rewards are significant. Forgiving opens the door to healing, growth, and personal evolution. On the other hand, holding onto grudges can profoundly affect your emotional, mental, and physical health. It can weigh heavily on your mental well-being, resulting in heightened levels of stress, anxiety, and depression. Furthermore, it can impact your physical health, as research suggests that unforgiveness is correlated with elevated blood pressure, compromised immune systems, and heightened risk of heart disease.

Moreover, holding grudges can poison your relationships, hindering genuine connections and intimacy. It traps you in negativity, preventing you from experiencing joy, peace, and happiness.

The Healing Power of Forgiveness

Forgiveness has the power to heal emotional wounds and free you from the pain of the past. When you choose to forgive, you're not denying or downplaying your pain. Instead, you're acknowledging it and choosing to release it. Forgiveness enables you to release the negative emotions that hinder your progress, thereby making room for healing, personal development, and emotional wellness. Scientific studies indicate that forgiveness can enhance both mental and physical well-being. It diminishes stress and anxiety levels, decreases blood pressure, and enhances immune system function. Additionally, it enhances relationships by fostering empathy, understanding, and compassion. By forgiving, you set off a positive ripple effect in your life and the lives of those around you.

Steps to Practice Forgiveness

Embracing forgiveness is a journey that demands time, introspection, and commitment. Below are practical steps to nurture forgiveness in your life:

1. **Recognize the Impact:** Reflect on how holding onto grudges has affected your emotional state, relationships, and overall happiness. Acknowledge the burden it places on your heart and the liberation that comes with letting go.

2. **Shift Your Perspective:** Try to see the situation from a different viewpoint. Empathize with the other person's motivations or circumstances, understanding

that it doesn't excuse their actions but can foster empathy and broader understanding.

3. Practice Self-Compassion: Understand that forgiveness doesn't mean denying your pain. Recognize your emotions and grant yourself permission to heal. Treat yourself with kindness, patience, and understanding throughout the forgiveness process.

4. Release Resentment and Anger: Let go of negative emotions through techniques like writing unsent letters, engaging in therapeutic practices such as meditation or deep breathing, or seeking professional support through therapy or counseling.

Forgiveness, a catalyst for personal growth and healing, liberates you from emotional burdens, creating room for transformation. It's not about condoning or forgetting but about reclaiming peace of mind and breaking free from past pain.

Whether forgiving others or yourself, the journey involves self-reflection, empathy, and a dedication to personal well-being. By embracing forgiveness, you can break the cycle of pain and find inner healing.

Forgiveness is a nuanced and deeply individual journey, rooted in empathy and comprehension. Empathy enables us to step into another's shoes, facilitating the release of anger and resentment. It acknowledges the human capacity for growth and change, recognizing that mistakes are part of our shared experience.

Central to forgiveness is the understanding that it doesn't justify actions or erase past events. Rather, it's a conscious decision to relinquish negative emotions and reclaim inner peace. By forgiving, we detach ourselves from the grip of past grievances without condoning the behavior.

To nurture empathy and understanding, active listening is key. Engage in genuine dialogue, seeking to comprehend the other person's viewpoint without immediate judgment. This doesn't necessitate agreement, but it fosters a mindset conducive to compassion and forgiveness.

The Healing Power of Forgiveness for Mental and Physical Well-being

Forgiveness is instrumental in repairing and fortifying relationships. Grudges erect barriers between individuals, hindering growth and connection. Through forgiveness, these barriers dissolve, fostering an environment of healing and mutual understanding.

Transparent communication is pivotal in fostering forgiveness within relationships. Honest expression of emotions creates space for empathy and reconciliation to flourish.

Patience is paramount in the forgiveness process. Healing unfolds gradually, requiring time and understanding from both parties. Rushing the process can impede genuine reconciliation.

Embracing Forgiveness for Personal Growth and Wellness

Forgiveness transcends relationship repair, profoundly impacting mental and physical health. Research underscores its role in reducing stress, anxiety, and depression, fostering overall emotional well-being.

Unforgiveness takes a toll on our physical health as well, manifesting in conditions like high blood pressure and weakened immune function. Forgiveness alleviates these physical symptoms, promoting better health and vitality.

Moreover, forgiveness enriches interpersonal connections, cultivating love, compassion, and understanding. These benefits extend beyond personal relationships, enriching various facets of life including work and social interactions.

CHAPTER 8

HOW TO NAVIGATE AND EMBRACE LIFE'S TRANSITIONS

Navigating life's various transitions, whether it's marriage, relocation, career shifts, or retirement, can be a challenging journey for anyone, regardless of age, gender, ethnicity, or profession. Embracing change during these significant life shifts is a common struggle many people face.

Sometimes, you find yourself entering exciting new chapters you've planned for, yet the experience may not match your expectations. Other times, unexpected life events may throw you off course, leaving you feeling disoriented. Life's journey is unpredictable, filled with highs and lows that can leave you feeling dizzy.

So, how do we move forward?

Robert Frost's wisdom rings true: the only way out is through. Despite the difficulty and uncertainty, facing these transitions head-on is necessary to emerge stronger. Learning to accept where you are in each phase and adapting accordingly is a valuable skill.

First, acknowledge your emotions without apology. Life's curveballs can elicit a range of feelings, from excitement to anxiety. Understanding your emotions helps you navigate the transition more smoothly.

Direct your attention to what you can manage amid turbulent circumstances. While you may not control every aspect of a situation, identifying the things you can influence can provide a sense of stability. Whether it's researching a new city before a move or setting achievable goals, small actions can make a big difference.

Seek support from those who understand your experience. Sharing your struggles with trusted friends or family members who have been through similar transitions can provide invaluable guidance and comfort.

Remember, transitions are temporary. Embrace the lessons each phase brings and trust that brighter days lie ahead. By approaching life's transitions with an open mind and heart, you'll find beauty on the other side.

CONCLUSION

In this final chapter, we have recognized that emotional maturity is not a destination but a journey a continual process of growth, self-discovery, and learning. Throughout this book, we've explored the various facets of emotional maturity, from self-awareness and self-regulation to empathy and interpersonal skills. We've descended into the societal expectations and personal barriers that women often face on their path to emotional maturity, highlighting the importance of self-compassion and authenticity.

As we conclude, let us remember that emotional maturity is not about being perfect or having all the answers. It's about embracing our imperfections, acknowledging our vulnerabilities, and being willing to learn from our experiences. It's about cultivating resilience in the face of challenges and cultivating empathy in our interactions with others.

I encourage you to continue your journey towards emotional maturity with courage and curiosity. Keep exploring, keep growing, and keep embracing the complexity of your emotions. Remember that you are not alone on this journey there is a community of women supporting you, cheering you on, and walking alongside you. Together, we can create a world where emotional maturity is celebrated and valued in all its forms.